MIND-BLOWING HOCKEY FACTS

100 Incredible Stories from Hockey's Most Unbelievable Moments

FELIX GRAYSON

Copyright © 2025 by MindSpark Publishing

All rights reserved. No part of this book may be reproduced, stored in a retrieval system, or transmitted in any form or by any means—electronic, mechanical, photocopying, recording, or otherwise—without the prior written permission of the publisher, except in the case of brief quotations embodied in critical articles or reviews.

This book is intended to provide general information on the topics discussed and is not intended as a substitute for professional advice. Every effort has been made to ensure accuracy, but the author and publisher assume no responsibility for errors, omissions, or contrary interpretation of the subject matter.

Published by MindSpark Publishing.
Cover design by MindSpark Publishing.

CONTENTS

Before We Dive In... 8
Introduction 10
The Coldest Game Ever Played 13
The Stanley Cup's Wild Ride 15
The Goalie Who Played Without a Mask 17
The Zamboni Driver Who Became an NHL Goalie 19
The Curse of the Presidents' Trophy 21
The Octopus Tradition 23
The Fastest Hat Trick in NHL History 25
The Stanley Cup Once Lived in a Pool 27
The Emergency Goalie Rule 29
The Stanley Cup's Midnight Snack 31
The Puck That Vanished 33
The Time a Player Was Traded for Himself 35
The Only Goalie to Ever Score a Playoff Goal 37
The NHL Team That Forgot Their Jerseys 39
The Game That Ended in a Tie... After 6 Overtimes! 41
The Player Who Wore His Skates to Bed 43
The Mascot That Got Arrested 45
The Player Who Was Traded for a Bus 47
The Stanley Cup Was Once Left at a Bar 49
The Time the Puck Exploded 51
The Goalie Who Scored on His Own Net 53

The Player Who Wore a Mic and Regretted It 55

The NHL Game That Started with a Brawl 57

The Stanley Cup Was Once Used as a Flower Pot 59

The Time a Fan Stole the Puck... Mid-Game! 61

The Player Who Wore the Wrong Skates 63

The Game with Three Overtime Winners 65

The Team That Scored on Themselves Twice 67

The Goalie Who Played Every Game... for Seven Years! 69

The Stanley Cup Was Once Used as a Toilet 71

The Referee Who Scored a Goal 73

The Player Who Won the Stanley Cup Before Playing a Game 75

The Goalie Who Scored... Twice! 77

The Stanley Cup's Strange Travels 79

The Player with No Teeth 81

The Game Played Without a Puck 83

The Rookie Who Won MVP 85

The Fastest Slap Shot Ever Recorded 87

The Player Who Won the Stanley Cup... on a Broken Leg 89

The Coach Who Pulled His Own Goalie in Overtime 91

The Game That Used 132 Pucks 93

The Player Who Played for Two Teams in One Day 95

The Time an NHL Team Played with No Fans 97

The Time a Zamboni Caught Fire 99

The Shortest NHL Career Ever 101

The Fan Who Scored a Goal 103

The Goalie Who Played Without Pads 105

The Coach Who Climbed into the Stands 107

The Player Who Scored a Goal with His Face 109

The Player Who Forgot How to Get Dressed 111

The Time an NHL Team Played with No Goalie 113

The Player Who Scored Six Goals… and Lost 115

The Time an NHL Game Had No Penalties 117

The Player Who Played 29 Seasons 119

The Player Who Wore 22 Different Jersey Numbers 121

The Fastest NHL Suspension Ever 123

The Player Who Played 80 Games in a 78-Game Season 125

The Time an NHL Team Didn't Take a Single Shot 127

The Mascot That Got Banned 129

The Time a Team Scored Two Goals at Once 131

The Goalie Who Played Every Position 133

The Stanley Cup Was Once Stolen 135

The Time a Player Took 67 Penalty Minutes in One Game 137

The Game That Used Seven Goalies 139

The Player with the Most Teeth Lost 141

The Puck That Got Stuck in a Goalie's Pads 143

The Time a Zamboni Driver Crashed into the Boards 145

The Player Who Scored 10 Points in One Game 147

The Coach Who Benched His Entire Team 149

The Fastest Goal in NHL History 151

The Stanley Cup Was Drop-Kicked Off a Balcony 153

The Longest NHL Suspension Ever 155

The Goalie Who Scored His Own Goal… in Overtime 157

The Player Who Played Without a Stick 159

The Referee Who Forgot His Whistle 161

The Player Who Played with a Broken Skate 163

The Player Who Forgot His Jersey 165

The Game with No Stoppages 167

The Player Who Scored 500 Goals… Without a Hat Trick 169

The Goalie Who Wore the Wrong Jersey 171

The Time the Puck Got Stuck in a Goalie's Pants 173

The Team That Won a Game Without Taking a Shot 175

The Game with Three Goalie Assists 177

The Player Who Played for Two Teams in One Playoff 179

The Fastest Four Goals in NHL History 181

The Player Who Played with a Broken Jaw 183

The Time an NHL Game Was Delayed by a Bat 185

The Team That Scored on Their Own Empty Net 187

The Player Who Took a Penalty While on the Bench 189

The Time a Goalie Played Without a Mask 191

The Player Who Scored While Sitting Down 193

The Game That Ended in Fog 195

The Goalie Who Played Without a Stick 197

The Player Who Scored on His Own Penalty Shot 199

The Time a Player Scored a Goal with His Head 201

The Time a Player Scored with a Broken Stick 203

The Player Who Scored Five Goals Five Different Ways 205

The Game That Lasted Three Days 207

The Player Who Scored His First Goal Into His Own Net 209

The Stanley Cup That Got Left at the Airport 211
Conclusion 212
Acknowledgements 214
About the Author 216

BEFORE WE DIVE IN...

Did you know that this is just **one** of many **mind-blowing** books waiting to be discovered?

What if I told you there's a **world of jaw-dropping, unbelievable, and downright bizarre facts** across **sports, science, history, mysteries, and more**—each one packed with stories that will **challenge what you thought you knew?**

EVER WONDERED WHAT IT'S LIKE TO...

- Witness **record-breaking Olympic moments** that defy human limits?

- Explore **real-life conspiracy theories** that sound too wild to be true?

- Discover **unsolved mysteries** that still leave experts baffled?

- Learn about **billionaires, stock market**

crashes, and money secrets?

- Find out how **robots, AI, and space travel are shaping the future?**

- Experience the **most extreme sports, legendary battles, and shocking events?**

This is just the beginning. The **100 Mind-Blowing series** covers it **all.**

WANT TO SEE WHAT'S NEXT?

Go to **FelixGrayson.com** and explore the **growing collection** of books and audiobooks that will **entertain, amaze, and keep you coming back for more.**

Curiosity doesn't stop here—this is just the beginning. What will blow your mind next?

INTRODUCTION

Welcome to **100 Mind-Blowing Hockey Facts**, a collection guaranteed to make you say, **"No way, that actually happened?"** From outrageous plays to unbelievable records, this book is packed with stories that will make you see hockey in a whole new light.

Have you ever wondered what happens when a **Zamboni driver becomes an NHL goalie—and wins?** Or how a team managed to **score on their own empty net… by accident?** What about the time a game had to be **stopped because of thick fog covering the ice?** These are just a few of the **wild, unpredictable, and downright shocking** moments waiting for you inside. Each fact has been carefully chosen to **surprise, entertain, and make you appreciate just how crazy hockey can be.**

Whether you're a die-hard fan, a casual viewer, or just here for some **hockey trivia gold**, this book has something for everyone. Read it straight through, or flip to a random page and **let the surprises hit you like an open-ice check.** There's no wrong way to enjoy this journey through the **strangest, funniest, and most unbelievable moments in hockey history.**

So lace up your skates, grab your favorite rink-side snack, and get ready to **dive into the madness.** By the end, you might just have a few mind-blowing hockey stories of your own to share. **Let's drop the puck!**

Mind-Blowing Hockey Fact #1

MIND-BLOWING HOCKEY FACT #1

THE COLDEST GAME EVER PLAYED

The coldest outdoor NHL game on record was played in temperatures so brutal, players' water bottles **froze solid!**

On November 22, 2003, the Edmonton Oilers and Montreal Canadiens faced off in the **Heritage Classic** at Commonwealth Stadium in Edmonton. The temperature at puck drop? **-22°C (-8°F), with a wind chill of -30°C (-22°F)!** Despite the bitter cold, over **57,000 fans** packed the stadium, bundled in layers to witness history. Players had to wear toques over their helmets, and goalies reported their **masks freezing to their faces!**

Mind-Blowing Hockey Fact #2

MIND-BLOWING HOCKEY FACT #2

THE STANLEY CUP'S WILD RIDE

The Stanley Cup has been **lost, stolen, and even thrown into a fire**—but it just won't quit!

Over the years, the most famous trophy in sports has had some **bizarre adventures**. In 1905, members of the Ottawa Silver Seven celebrated by **kicking the Cup into a frozen canal**—they retrieved it the next day. In 1940, the New York Rangers **burned their mortgage papers inside it**, accidentally scorching the inside of the trophy. And in 1994, after the Rangers won again, **it was left on the side of the road after a night of partying!** Despite all the chaos, the Stanley Cup **always finds its way back home.**

Mind-Blowing Hockey Fact #3

MIND-BLOWING HOCKEY FACT #3

THE GOALIE WHO PLAYED WITHOUT A MASK

The last NHL goalie to play without a mask did it for **years—even after taking pucks to the face!**

Jacques Plante of the Montreal Canadiens became the **first goalie to wear a mask regularly in 1959, but not everyone followed his lead right away.** The last NHL goalie to go maskless was **Andy Brown**, who played for the Pittsburgh Penguins in **1974—yes, 15 years after Plante's breakthrough!** Brown took countless shots to the face, regularly needing stitches mid-game. His reasoning? He believed a mask **would block his vision.** Thankfully, today's goalies aren't making the same sacrifice!

Mind-Blowing Hockey Fact #4

MIND-BLOWING HOCKEY FACT #4

THE ZAMBONI DRIVER WHO BECAME AN NHL GOALIE

A 42-year-old **Zamboni driver** was forced into action—and won an NHL game!

On February 22, 2020, the Carolina Hurricanes faced a **goalie crisis** when both of their netminders got injured. Enter **David Ayres**, a **Zamboni driver and emergency backup goalie** who had never played in the NHL. Despite giving up **two quick goals**, Ayres settled in and **shut the door**, leading Carolina to a **6-3 victory** over the Toronto Maple Leafs. He became the **first emergency backup in NHL history to record a win**—earning the locker room celebration of a lifetime!

Mind-Blowing Hockey Fact #5

MIND-BLOWING HOCKEY FACT #5

THE CURSE OF THE PRESIDENTS' TROPHY

Winning the **Presidents' Trophy** is supposed to be a good thing—except it usually isn't.

The trophy is awarded to the NHL team with the **best regular-season record**, but history has shown that this "honor" often comes with a **mysterious curse.** Since its introduction in 1985, **less than 25%** of Presidents' Trophy winners have gone on to win the **Stanley Cup.** Some of the best teams in history have dominated the regular season, only to collapse in the playoffs—including the **2019 Tampa Bay Lightning,** who were **swept in the first round after a record-breaking season!**

Mind-Blowing Hockey Fact #6

MIND-BLOWING HOCKEY FACT #6

THE OCTOPUS TRADITION

Detroit Red Wings fans **throw octopuses onto the ice**—and it's been happening for decades!

This bizarre tradition started in **1952**, when two brothers tossed an **octopus onto the ice** at a Red Wings playoff game. Back then, teams needed **eight wins to capture the Stanley Cup**—one for each tentacle. The Red Wings won the Cup that year, and the tradition stuck! Over the years, fans have hurled octopuses of all sizes onto the ice, with the **largest ever** weighing a whopping **50 pounds!** The NHL has tried to ban it, but Detroit fans refuse to let the tradition die.

Mind-Blowing Hockey Fact #7

MIND-BLOWING HOCKEY FACT #7

THE FASTEST HAT TRICK IN NHL HISTORY

One player scored **three goals in just 21 seconds—an NHL record that still stands!**

On March 23, 1952, **Bill Mosienko** of the Chicago Blackhawks pulled off the **fastest hat trick in NHL history,** scoring **three goals in just 21 seconds** against the New York Rangers. The most shocking part? His linemate **set up all three goals in the same shift!** To this day, no one has come close to breaking Mosienko's record—making it one of the most **mind-blowing moments in hockey history.**

Mind-Blowing Hockey Fact #8

THE STANLEY CUP ONCE LIVED IN A POOL

One NHL player casually **left the Stanley Cup at the bottom of his swimming pool!**

After winning the Cup in 1994, **Ed Belfour** of the Dallas Stars decided to **give the trophy a swim.** Instead of keeping it on display, he **dropped it into his pool** and left it sitting at the bottom! This wasn't the only time the Cup has taken a dip—other players have bathed their **dogs, babies, and even champagne** in it. But Belfour's decision to use it as a **makeshift pool ornament** is one of the wildest Cup stories ever.

Mind-Blowing Hockey Fact #9

MIND-BLOWING HOCKEY FACT #9

THE EMERGENCY GOALIE RULE

An NHL team can use **anyone** as an emergency goalie—including a fan from the stands!

Unlike other positions, NHL teams only dress **two goalies per game**, meaning that if both get injured, they need an **emergency backup**—even if that means grabbing a **random guy from the crowd!** This rule has led to **wild moments**, like in 2018 when **Scott Foster**, a 36-year-old accountant, was called in to play for the Chicago Blackhawks. Despite having **zero NHL experience**, he **stopped all seven shots he faced** and became an overnight legend!

Mind-Blowing Hockey Fact #10

MIND-BLOWING HOCKEY FACT #10

THE STANLEY CUP'S MIDNIGHT SNACK

One player ate **spaghetti and meatballs** straight out of the Stanley Cup!

After winning the Stanley Cup, players get **one day with the trophy**—and they've done some bizarre things with it. In **1996**, Colorado Avalanche captain **Joe Sakic** filled the Cup with **spaghetti and meatballs** and ate right out of it like a giant bowl! Other players have filled it with **ice cream, cereal, and even dog food** for their pets. The Cup has seen it all—but Sakic's pasta dinner remains one of the most legendary meals ever eaten from hockey's greatest prize.

Mind-Blowing Hockey Fact #11

MIND-BLOWING HOCKEY FACT #11

THE PUCK THAT VANISHED

An NHL goal was scored—**but the puck completely disappeared!**

During a game in **2017**, the St. Louis Blues scored against the Toronto Maple Leafs, but there was just **one problem**—no one could find the puck! Replays showed that after crossing the goal line, the puck **slipped through a hole in the net** and vanished under the boards. The refs were **completely baffled**, and the game had to be paused while they searched for it. Eventually, the goal was confirmed, but the mystery of the **missing puck** left everyone stunned!

Mind-Blowing Hockey Fact #12

MIND-BLOWING HOCKEY FACT #12

THE TIME A PLAYER WAS TRADED FOR HIMSELF

An NHL player was **traded for himself**—yes, really!

In 1987, **Brent Gretzky** (Wayne Gretzky's younger brother) was part of a **"future considerations" trade** between the Quebec Nordiques and the Minnesota North Stars. Months later, when the teams finalized the deal, Quebec ended up **reacquiring Gretzky**—essentially **trading him back for himself!** This bizarre situation remains one of the **weirdest transactions** in NHL history.

Mind-Blowing Hockey Fact #13

MIND-BLOWING HOCKEY FACT #13

THE ONLY GOALIE TO EVER SCORE A PLAYOFF GOAL

A goalie **once scored a goal in the Stanley Cup Playoffs**—something no other goalie has ever done!

On April 17, 1997, **Martin Brodeur** of the New Jersey Devils made history by becoming **the first and only NHL goalie to score a goal in a playoff game.** With the opposing team's net empty, Brodeur fired the puck down the ice, and it slid perfectly into the goal. While several goalies have scored in the regular season, **Brodeur's playoff goal remains a one-of-a-kind achievement.**

Mind-Blowing Hockey Fact #14

MIND-BLOWING HOCKEY FACT #14

THE NHL TEAM THAT FORGOT THEIR JERSEYS

An NHL team **once had to wear their opponents' practice jerseys** because they forgot their own!

In 2008, the **Los Angeles Kings** traveled to play the Vancouver Canucks, but when they arrived at the arena, they realized **they had forgotten to pack their jerseys.** With no time to get them, the Kings had no choice but to borrow **white practice jerseys from the Canucks.** The game went on as scheduled, but it was a bizarre sight—**an entire NHL team playing in the wrong uniforms!**

Mind-Blowing Hockey Fact #15

MIND-BLOWING HOCKEY FACT #15

THE GAME THAT ENDED IN A TIE... AFTER 6 OVERTIMES!

One NHL playoff game **lasted over 176 minutes**—and still didn't have a winner!

On March 24, 1936, the **Detroit Red Wings and Montreal Maroons** played the **longest game in NHL history.** The game went into an exhausting **six overtimes**, lasting **176 minutes and 30 seconds** before Detroit's **Muddy Ruel** finally scored the game-winning goal. By the time it ended, players were **collapsing from exhaustion**, goalies had faced over **90 shots**, and the ice was a mess. It remains the **longest game in NHL history**—and may never be broken!

Mind-Blowing Hockey Fact #16

MIND-BLOWING HOCKEY FACT #16

THE PLAYER WHO WORE HIS SKATES TO BED

One NHL player was so dedicated, he **slept in his skates as a kid!**

Hall of Famer **Glenn Hall**, one of the greatest goalies in NHL history, had an unusual way of preparing for his career—**he wore his skates to bed** as a child! Growing up on a farm in Canada, Hall wanted to **break in his skates faster**, so he slept with them on to mold them to his feet. His dedication paid off—he went on to set an NHL record by playing **502 consecutive games as a goalie**—without a mask!

Mind-Blowing Hockey Fact #17

MIND-BLOWING HOCKEY FACT #17

THE MASCOT THAT GOT ARRESTED

An NHL mascot was **once arrested—on the ice!**

During the 2001 NHL All-Star Game in Denver, the **San Jose Sharks' mascot, S.J. Sharkie**, attempted a **dramatic entrance** by rappelling from the rafters. But things went horribly wrong when he got **stuck in midair**, dangling helplessly above the ice. Firefighters had to rescue him, but the chaos didn't stop there—**security officers then "arrested" him for disrupting the event!** While it was mostly for laughs, **S.J. Sharkie remains the only NHL mascot to ever be "arrested" at a game!**

Mind-Blowing Hockey Fact #18

MIND-BLOWING HOCKEY FACT #18

THE PLAYER WHO WAS TRADED FOR A BUS

An NHL player was once **traded for a bus—yes, an actual bus!**

In 1993, minor league player **Tom Martin** was traded from the Victoria Cougars to the Seattle Breakers in exchange for a **brand-new team bus.** The Cougars desperately needed new transportation, and instead of cash or draft picks, they **traded away Martin to cover the cost!** Luckily, he took it in stride, later joking that he hoped he was at least worth **a luxury model.**

Mind-Blowing Hockey Fact #19

MIND-BLOWING HOCKEY FACT #19

THE STANLEY CUP WAS ONCE LEFT AT A BAR

The most prized trophy in hockey was **once forgotten at a bar—overnight!**

After winning the **1924 Stanley Cup**, members of the Montreal Canadiens took the trophy out for a celebratory dinner. But as the night went on, excitement took over, and **they accidentally left it behind at the bar!** The next morning, they scrambled back to retrieve it, finding the Cup **right where they had left it.** Luckily, no one had stolen it—**but it definitely had one wild night!**

Mind-Blowing Hockey Fact #20

MIND-BLOWING HOCKEY FACT #20

THE TIME THE PUCK EXPLODED

An NHL puck **once shattered into pieces during a game!**

During a **1979** game between the St. Louis Blues and the New York Rangers, the puck **literally exploded** after being hit with a powerful slap shot. The frozen rubber couldn't handle the impact, and it **shattered into multiple pieces** on the ice! The refs had to **pause the game** while players picked up the broken fragments. Though rare, exploding pucks have happened a few times—especially in **extremely cold conditions** when the rubber becomes brittle!

Mind-Blowing Hockey Fact #21

MIND-BLOWING HOCKEY FACT #21

THE GOALIE WHO SCORED ON HIS OWN NET

A goalie once **scored an own-goal—without even touching the puck!**

In **2013**, Phoenix Coyotes goalie **Mike Smith** became the **first NHL netminder to lose a game by scoring on himself in overtime.** During a matchup against the Buffalo Sabres, an opponent dumped the puck into the zone, and it **bounced weirdly off the boards.** The puck hit Smith's **back**, trickled into the net, and the game was over. Since the last Buffalo player to touch the puck was the official scorer, **Smith was credited with the goal against his own team!**

Mind-Blowing Hockey Fact #22

MIND-BLOWING HOCKEY FACT #22

THE PLAYER WHO WORE A MIC AND REGRETTED IT

An NHL player was **mic'd up—only to get injured moments later!**

During the **1993 Stanley Cup Final**, Los Angeles Kings star **Wayne Gretzky** convinced teammate **Marty McSorley** to wear a microphone for a live broadcast. Just minutes into the game, McSorley took a **brutal hit**, and his **painful groans were caught on live TV!** The NHL quickly reconsidered its approach to **mic'd-up players**, realizing that broadcasting **real-time agony** wasn't the best idea.

Mind-Blowing Hockey Fact #23

MIND-BLOWING HOCKEY FACT #23

THE NHL GAME THAT STARTED WITH A BRAWL

An NHL game once began with **a full-team fight—before the puck even dropped!**

On **December 23, 1991**, the New York Rangers and Quebec Nordiques took pre-game tension to another level. As soon as the referee **got ready for the opening faceoff**, players from both teams **dropped their gloves and started fighting!** The game hadn't even officially started, yet **all 10 skaters on the ice were already throwing punches.** It remains one of the most **chaotic** starts to an NHL game in history!

Mind-Blowing Hockey Fact #24

MIND-BLOWING HOCKEY FACT #24

THE STANLEY CUP WAS ONCE USED AS A FLOWER POT

A hockey fan **once planted flowers in the Stanley Cup—without realizing what it was!**

In **1905**, after the Ottawa Silver Seven won the Stanley Cup, one player **brought it home and left it in his backyard.** A few days later, his mother, not recognizing the legendary trophy, **filled it with dirt and planted flowers in it!** The Cup sat as a **makeshift flower pot** until the team realized what had happened and retrieved it. This remains one of the **strangest Stanley Cup mishaps in history!**

Mind-Blowing Hockey Fact #25

MIND-BLOWING HOCKEY FACT #25

THE TIME A FAN STOLE THE PUCK... MID-GAME!

A fan once **snatched the puck off the ice—while the game was still going!**

During a **2001** game between the New York Islanders and the Tampa Bay Lightning, a loose puck slid toward the boards. Before a player could retrieve it, a **fan reached over the glass, grabbed the puck, and hid it in his jacket!** The referees were **completely confused**, looking around for the missing puck while the fan sat there **acting innocent.** He was eventually caught and had to return the puck—but not before delaying the game with one of the **boldest fan moves in NHL history!**

Mind-Blowing Hockey Fact #26

THE PLAYER WHO WORE THE WRONG SKATES

An NHL player **once played an entire game wearing someone else's skates—by accident!**

During a game in **1970**, Boston Bruins defenseman **Bobby Orr** was in a rush to get dressed and **accidentally put on his teammate's skates.** Despite the mix-up, he still **dominated the game**, scoring a goal and adding an assist. When he realized the mistake afterward, Orr just **shrugged it off**, proving that for a legend like him, even the wrong equipment couldn't slow him down!

Mind-Blowing Hockey Fact #27

MIND-BLOWING HOCKEY FACT #27

THE GAME WITH THREE OVERTIME WINNERS

An NHL game once had **three different** **"game-winning"** goals—because two were **disallowed**!

During a **2013 playoff game** between the Chicago Blackhawks and Los Angeles Kings, the Blackhawks thought they had won in overtime—not once, but **twice**. Both goals were **reviewed and overturned**, leaving fans in disbelief. Finally, on the **third attempt**, Chicago's **Brent Seabrook** scored the **real** game-winner, sealing the victory for good. It was one of the **wildest finishes in playoff history**, proving that sometimes, winning takes more than just one shot!

Mind-Blowing Hockey Fact #28

THE TEAM THAT SCORED ON THEMSELVES TWICE

One NHL team **accidentally scored two own-goals in the same game—and still won!**

During a **1976 game**, the Colorado Rockies (now the New Jersey Devils) pulled off the impossible—**they scored on themselves twice in one night!** The bizarre goals happened when defensemen attempted to clear the puck but ended up **shooting it straight into their own net.** Despite these massive blunders, the Rockies still **managed to win the game**, proving that sometimes, even a little self-sabotage isn't enough to stop a victory!

Mind-Blowing Hockey Fact #29

MIND-BLOWING HOCKEY FACT #29

THE GOALIE WHO PLAYED EVERY GAME... FOR SEVEN YEARS!

One NHL goalie played **every single game for seven straight seasons**—without missing a single start!

From **1955 to 1962, Glenn Hall** of the Chicago Blackhawks played an **unbelievable 502 consecutive games**, all **without wearing a mask!** Nicknamed **"Mr. Goalie"**, Hall endured **puck bruises, exhaustion, and even playing through sickness**—yet he never took a night off. His streak is considered **one of the toughest records in NHL history**, and with today's goalie rotations, it will likely **never be broken!**

Mind-Blowing Hockey Fact #30

MIND-BLOWING HOCKEY FACT #30

THE STANLEY CUP WAS ONCE USED AS A TOILET

A baby **once used the Stanley Cup as a toilet—seriously!**

After the **1905 Ottawa Silver Seven's Stanley Cup win**, a player brought the trophy home, where his **toddler decided to use it as a potty!** Decades later, after the **1994 New York Rangers' victory, Brian Leetch's son did the exact same thing!** While the Cup has been used for **champagne, cereal, and even dog food**, this might be the **strangest (and messiest) use of all!**

Mind-Blowing Hockey Fact #31

MIND-BLOWING HOCKEY FACT #31

THE REFEREE WHO SCORED A GOAL

An NHL referee **once accidentally scored a goal—against his own team!**

During a game in **1980**, a shot from the blue line **bounced off referee Ron Foyt's skate** and slid into the net. The problem? The goal counted **against the team he was standing near!** Since referees are considered **part of the play**, the unlucky bounce was ruled a **good goal**. The players were furious, but the bizarre moment proved that sometimes, even the refs can change the outcome of a game!

Mind-Blowing Hockey Fact #32

MIND-BLOWING HOCKEY FACT #32

THE PLAYER WHO WON THE STANLEY CUP BEFORE PLAYING A GAME

One player **became a Stanley Cup champion before ever playing in the NHL!**

In **2011, Tomas Tatar** was called up by the Detroit Red Wings but didn't play in a single NHL game that season. However, because he was part of the **Black Aces** (a group of reserve players teams carry in the playoffs), he still got his **name engraved on the Stanley Cup** when Detroit won! He went on to have a solid NHL career, but Tatar holds the rare honor of being a **Stanley Cup winner before ever stepping on NHL ice!**

100 MIND-BLOWING HOCKEY FACTS

Mind-Blowing Hockey Fact #33

MIND-BLOWING HOCKEY FACT #33

THE GOALIE WHO SCORED... TWICE!

One NHL goalie **scored two goals in his career**—a record that still stands!

While goalies rarely get the chance to score, **Ron Hextall** of the Philadelphia Flyers did it twice! In **1987**, he became the **first NHL goalie to score by shooting the puck into the empty net**. Then, in **1989**, he did it **again—this time in a playoff game!** Hextall's offensive skills made him **the first netminder in history with multiple career goals**, a record that has yet to be broken!

Mind-Blowing Hockey Fact #34

MIND-BLOWING HOCKEY FACT #34

THE STANLEY CUP'S STRANGE TRAVELS

The Stanley Cup has been **to war zones, mountaintops, and even space!**

Over the years, the Cup has gone on some **wild adventures.** In 2004, it was taken to **a war zone in Afghanistan** to boost troop morale. It has also been to the **top of Mount Everest, the bottom of a swimming pool, and even inside a player's bed!** But its most mind-blowing trip? In **2007**, astronaut **Garrett Reisman** took a **replica** of the Cup into **outer space!**

Mind-Blowing Hockey Fact #35

MIND-BLOWING HOCKEY FACT #35

THE PLAYER WITH NO TEETH

One NHL legend **played most of his career with barely any teeth!**

Bobby Clarke, the **Hall of Fame captain** of the Philadelphia Flyers, was known for his **fearless play and toothless grin.** Due to the rough style of hockey in the **1970s,** Clarke lost most of his front teeth early in his career—but he **refused to wear dentures on the ice!** Instead, he embraced his famous gap-toothed smile, making it one of the most **iconic looks in hockey history.**

Mind-Blowing Hockey Fact #36

MIND-BLOWING HOCKEY FACT #36

THE GAME PLAYED WITHOUT A PUCK

An NHL game **once started without a puck—because no one could find one!**

During a **1979 matchup**, the Montreal Canadiens and Pittsburgh Penguins were **ready for puck drop—except there was no puck!** The referees searched everywhere but couldn't find one, leading to an awkward delay. Eventually, an **arena staff member ran to grab a new puck**, and the game finally began. It's one of the rare moments where an NHL game was **stopped before it even started!**

Mind-Blowing Hockey Fact #37

MIND-BLOWING HOCKEY FACT #37

THE ROOKIE WHO WON MVP

A rookie **once won the NHL's MVP award—something no one else has done since!**

In **1939, Carl Voss** became the **only player in NHL history** to win the **Hart Trophy (league MVP) in his rookie season.** While many incredible rookies have made an impact over the years, **not even Wayne Gretzky, Mario Lemieux, or Sidney Crosby** managed to pull this off! Voss's achievement remains one of the **most unbreakable records in hockey history.**

Mind-Blowing Hockey Fact #38

MIND-BLOWING HOCKEY FACT #38

THE FASTEST SLAP SHOT EVER RECORDED

One NHL player blasted a **slap shot at a jaw-dropping 118 mph!**

During the **2012 NHL All-Star Skills Competition, Zdeno Chára** unleashed a **118.3 mph (190.4 km/h) slap shot**, setting the record for the **fastest shot in NHL history.** Chára, known for his towering **6'9" frame**, had already broken the record multiple times before finally reaching this insane speed. To this day, no player has been able to **top his legendary rocket of a shot!**

Mind-Blowing Hockey Fact #39

MIND-BLOWING HOCKEY FACT #39

THE PLAYER WHO WON THE STANLEY CUP... ON A BROKEN LEG

One NHL star **played through the Stanley Cup Final with a broken leg—and still scored the winning goal!**

In **1964, Bobby Baun** of the Toronto Maple Leafs suffered a **fractured ankle** in Game 6 of the Stanley Cup Final. Instead of sitting out, he **refused to leave the game,** had his leg **frozen with painkillers,** and came back to **score the game-winning goal in overtime!** The Leafs went on to win the Cup in Game 7, making Baun's heroic moment one of the **toughest performances in NHL history.**

Mind-Blowing Hockey Fact #40

THE COACH WHO PULLED HIS OWN GOALIE IN OVERTIME

One NHL coach **pulled his goalie in overtime—and it instantly backfired!**

During a **1998 game**, Buffalo Sabres coach **Lindy Ruff** made a **shocking decision**—he pulled his goalie in overtime while **on the power play**, hoping for a 6-on-3 advantage. Instead, the opposing team **immediately stole the puck and scored into the empty net!** The risky move **backfired in seconds**, making it one of the most bizarre coaching decisions in NHL history.

Mind-Blowing Hockey Fact #41

MIND-BLOWING HOCKEY FACT #41

THE GAME THAT USED 132 PUCKS

One NHL game **went through 132 pucks — because they kept freezing!**

During the **2003 Heritage Classic**, an outdoor game between the Edmonton Oilers and Montreal Canadiens, the temperature dropped to a **bone-chilling -22°C (-8°F), with a wind chill of -30°C (-22°F)**. Because of the extreme cold, the pucks **kept cracking and breaking**, forcing officials to **constantly swap them out**. By the end of the game, a record-breaking **132 pucks** had been used — something never seen before in NHL history!

Mind-Blowing Hockey Fact #42

MIND-BLOWING HOCKEY FACT #42

THE PLAYER WHO PLAYED FOR TWO TEAMS IN ONE DAY

One NHL player **played for two different teams—on the same day!**

On **March 10, 1991, goaltender Clint Malarchuk** started the day as a member of the **Quebec Nordiques**, playing against the Hartford Whalers. After the game, he was **traded to the Whalers**, who had a game that same night. Malarchuk suited up again, this time **playing for Hartford!** He remains one of the **only players in NHL history to play for two teams in a single day.**

Mind-Blowing Hockey Fact #43

MIND-BLOWING HOCKEY FACT #43

THE TIME AN NHL TEAM PLAYED WITH NO FANS

An NHL game was played **in front of an empty arena—with zero fans in attendance!**

On **April 26, 2020**, due to the **COVID-19 pandemic**, the NHL resumed play in a "bubble" environment, where games were played **without any spectators.** While it was a strange sight, it wasn't the first time an NHL team had played without fans. In **1992**, a game between the New Jersey Devils and Calgary Flames was postponed due to a **blizzard**, and when it finally resumed, **only a handful of fans could make it.** The announcers joked that it felt like **a scrimmage instead of an NHL game!**

Mind-Blowing Hockey Fact #44

MIND-BLOWING HOCKEY FACT #44

THE TIME A ZAMBONI CAUGHT FIRE

A Zamboni **burst into flames—while cleaning the ice!**

During a **2020** high school hockey game in Rochester, New York, a Zamboni was doing its usual resurfacing when it suddenly **caught on fire mid-rink!** The driver, miraculously unfazed, calmly finished resurfacing the ice **while flames shot out from the engine.** The fire was eventually put out, but the **image of a burning Zamboni rolling across the ice** became an instant internet sensation!

Mind-Blowing Hockey Fact #45

MIND-BLOWING HOCKEY FACT #45

THE SHORTEST NHL CAREER EVER

One NHL player's career **lasted just three seconds!**

On **March 22, 1948, Bobby Gassoff** of the St. Louis Blues was sent onto the ice for his NHL debut—but as soon as the puck dropped, a fight broke out. Gassoff was immediately **given a game misconduct** and ejected before he could even **take a single shift!** His official NHL career lasted just **three seconds**, making it the shortest in league history.

Mind-Blowing Hockey Fact #46

MIND-BLOWING HOCKEY FACT #46

THE FAN WHO SCORED A GOAL

A **fan once scored a goal in an NHL game—without stepping on the ice!**

During a **2016 game**, the St. Louis Blues took a shot that **missed the net** and deflected over the glass. The puck flew straight into the stands, where a fan sitting behind the goal **instinctively caught it and dropped it into his beer cup.** The cameras caught the moment perfectly, making it look like **the fan had "scored" a goal!** The crowd erupted, and even the players **laughed at the lucky shot.**

Mind-Blowing Hockey Fact #47

MIND-BLOWING HOCKEY FACT #47

THE GOALIE WHO PLAYED WITHOUT PADS

An NHL goalie **once played an entire game without proper leg pads!**

In **1927**, New York Rangers goalie **Lorne Chabot** had his leg pads **go missing before a game.** With no backup gear available, he was forced to **improvise**—so he **borrowed a pair of cricket pads from a nearby sports store!** Despite the awkward fit, Chabot still played the game, proving that hockey players will do **whatever it takes to stay on the ice!**

Mind-Blowing Hockey Fact #48

MIND-BLOWING HOCKEY FACT #48

THE COACH WHO CLIMBED INTO THE STANDS

An NHL coach **once left the bench mid-game—to fight a fan!**

During a **1979** game at Madison Square Garden, tensions boiled over when a fan **grabbed a player's hockey stick from the bench.** Furious, Boston Bruins head coach **Don Cherry** and several players **climbed into the stands**, sparking a wild brawl between the team and the fans! Security eventually broke it up, but the incident remains **one of the craziest moments in NHL history.**

Mind-Blowing Hockey Fact #49

MIND-BLOWING HOCKEY FACT #49

THE PLAYER WHO SCORED A GOAL WITH HIS FACE

An NHL player **once scored a goal using his face—by accident!**

During a **2009** game, Detroit Red Wings forward **Johan Franzen** went to the front of the net when a teammate took a powerful shot. The puck **deflected off Franzen's face** and went straight into the goal! While he was left with a **bloody nose and a swollen lip**, the goal still counted. When asked about it after the game, Franzen simply laughed and said, **"They all count, right?"**

Mind-Blowing Hockey Fact #50

MIND-BLOWING HOCKEY FACT #50

THE PLAYER WHO FORGOT HOW TO GET DRESSED

An NHL rookie **once had to ask a teammate for help putting on his gear!**

When **Sidney Crosby** entered the NHL in **2005**, he was just **18 years old** and had never worn **a suit of brand-new pro-level equipment.** On his first day, he struggled so much with his gear that veteran **Mario Lemieux** had to help him **lace up his skates and adjust his pads!** Despite the rough start, Crosby went on to become **one of the greatest players in NHL history.**

Mind-Blowing Hockey Fact #51

THE TIME AN NHL TEAM PLAYED WITH NO GOALIE

An NHL team **once had to play without a goalie for nearly the entire game!**

During a **1928 Stanley Cup Final** game, the New York Rangers' starting goalie **Lorne Chabot** suffered an eye injury. With no backup goalie on the roster, the team was forced to **put in their coach—Lester Patrick!** At **44 years old**, Patrick suited up and **somehow helped the Rangers win the game**, making him the **oldest goaltender to ever play in a Stanley Cup Final.**

Mind-Blowing Hockey Fact #52

MIND-BLOWING HOCKEY FACT #52

THE PLAYER WHO SCORED SIX GOALS... AND LOST

One player **once scored six goals in a single game—but his team still lost!**

On **January 31, 1920, Joe Malone** of the Quebec Bulldogs put on a historic performance, scoring **six goals** in a game against the Toronto St. Patricks. Despite his incredible effort, the Bulldogs **still lost the game 10-6!** Malone remains the **only player in NHL history to score six times in a game and still end up on the losing side.**

Mind-Blowing Hockey Fact #53

MIND-BLOWING HOCKEY FACT #53

THE TIME AN NHL GAME HAD NO PENALTIES

One NHL game was played **without a single penalty**—something that almost never happens!

On **October 8, 1977**, the **Toronto Maple Leafs and St. Louis Blues** played an entire **60-minute game** without a single **penalty being called**. In a sport known for its rough play and fights, this was almost unheard of! Since the NHL started tracking penalty stats in **1933**, fewer than **five games** have ever been completely penalty-free.

Mind-Blowing Hockey Fact #54

MIND-BLOWING HOCKEY FACT #54

THE PLAYER WHO PLAYED 29 SEASONS

One NHL legend **played professional hockey for an unbelievable 29 seasons!**

Gordie Howe, known as "Mr. Hockey," had one of the longest careers in sports history, playing **from 1946 to 1980**. He retired at 52 years old after playing in **five different decades!** Even more impressive, he played **alongside his own sons** in his final seasons. Howe's legendary toughness and longevity set a record that **no player has come close to breaking.**

Mind-Blowing Hockey Fact #55

MIND-BLOWING HOCKEY FACT #55

THE PLAYER WHO WORE 22 DIFFERENT JERSEY NUMBERS

One NHL player **wore 22 different jersey numbers throughout his career—a record!**

Journeyman forward **Mike Sillinger** played for an NHL-record **12 different teams**, meaning he had to constantly change jersey numbers. By the time he retired in **2009**, he had worn a staggering **22 different numbers**, more than any player in NHL history! No matter what number was on his back, Sillinger was known for his **versatility and leadership**, making an impact wherever he played.

Mind-Blowing Hockey Fact #56

THE FASTEST NHL SUSPENSION EVER

One NHL player **was suspended just nine seconds into his career!**

In **1987**, defenseman **Dave Manson** made his NHL debut for the Chicago Blackhawks. Just **nine seconds into his first shift**, he got into a fight and was handed a **game misconduct penalty.** The league reviewed the incident and **suspended him for the next game**, making it the fastest suspension ever given to a rookie!

Mind-Blowing Hockey Fact #57

MIND-BLOWING HOCKEY FACT #57

THE PLAYER WHO PLAYED 80 GAMES IN A 78-GAME SEASON

One NHL player **played more games than his own team in a single season!**

In **1992-93**, forward **Jimmy Carson** was traded from the Detroit Red Wings to the Los Angeles Kings mid-season. Because of scheduling differences, he ended up playing **a total of 80 games**—even though both teams only played **78 games that season!** Carson is one of the few players in NHL history to **play more games than the actual length of the season.**

Mind-Blowing Hockey Fact #58

MIND-BLOWING HOCKEY FACT #58

THE TIME AN NHL TEAM DIDN'T TAKE A SINGLE SHOT

One NHL team **once went an entire period without recording a single shot on goal!**

During a **2014 game**, the Toronto Maple Leafs faced the Columbus Blue Jackets and made history—but not in a good way. In the **second period**, the Leafs failed to record **a single shot on net**, despite playing the full **20 minutes**! It was one of the **few times in NHL history** that a team was completely shut down for an entire period, proving that even the best teams can have **off nights**.

Mind-Blowing Hockey Fact #59

MIND-BLOWING HOCKEY FACT #59

THE MASCOT THAT GOT BANNED

An NHL mascot was **once banned from the arena**—for being too wild!

During a **1999** game, the **Phoenix Coyotes' mascot, Howler the Coyote**, got a little too **enthusiastic** while hyping up the crowd. He climbed over the boards and **started banging on the glass behind the opposing team's bench**, distracting the players. The referees weren't amused and **ejected the mascot from the game**, effectively banning him from the ice for the night!

Mind-Blowing Hockey Fact #60

THE TIME A TEAM SCORED TWO GOALS AT ONCE

An NHL team **once scored two goals at the same time—accidentally!**

During a **1978 game**, the Colorado Rockies pulled their goalie for an extra attacker. As they pressured the opposing net, a Rockies player **shot the puck toward the goal—while at the same time, a delayed penalty was called against their opponents.** The puck went in, and just as the goal light flashed, the referee **also awarded a penalty shot!** The Rockies technically **scored two goals on one play,** but only one counted on the scoreboard!

Mind-Blowing Hockey Fact #61

MIND-BLOWING HOCKEY FACT #61

THE GOALIE WHO PLAYED EVERY POSITION

One NHL goalie **once played every single position—including forward!**

In **1928**, New York Rangers goalie **Chubby Charlie Rayner** found himself in a bizarre situation when his team suffered multiple injuries. With no substitutes left, he **took off his goalie pads and skated as a forward** for part of the game! While he didn't score, he remains **one of the only goalies in history** to officially play in net and as a skater in the same game.

Mind-Blowing Hockey Fact #62

MIND-BLOWING HOCKEY FACT #62

THE STANLEY CUP WAS ONCE STOLEN

The Stanley Cup **was once stolen—and missing for months!**

In **1962**, after the Toronto Maple Leafs won the Cup, the trophy was put on display in the **Hockey Hall of Fame in Montreal**. But one night, thieves **broke in and stole it!** The Cup mysteriously disappeared for **three months** before being found abandoned at a **police station parking lot**. To this day, no one knows who took it or why they decided to return it!

Mind-Blowing Hockey Fact #63

THE TIME A PLAYER TOOK 67 PENALTY MINUTES IN ONE GAME

One NHL player **once racked up 67 penalty minutes in a single game!**

During a **1992 game**, tough guy **Randy Holt** of the Los Angeles Kings completely lost his temper and set an **NHL record for most penalty minutes in one game.** Holt was involved in multiple fights, received **a game misconduct, a 10-minute misconduct, and multiple minors**, all adding up to an unbelievable **67 minutes in penalties!** No player has even come close to breaking this chaotic record.

Mind-Blowing Hockey Fact #64

MIND-BLOWING HOCKEY FACT #64

THE GAME THAT USED SEVEN GOALIES

One NHL game **featured a record seven different goalies!**

On **March 10, 1982**, the Boston Bruins and Minnesota North Stars played a game that quickly turned into **goalie chaos.** Due to injuries and poor performances, a **record-setting seven different goalies** played in a single game! With teams running out of options, even backup goalies who rarely saw the ice were forced into action, making it one of the **strangest games in NHL history.**

Mind-Blowing Hockey Fact #65

MIND-BLOWING HOCKEY FACT #65

THE PLAYER WITH THE MOST TEETH LOST

One NHL player **lost all but three teeth during his career!**

Hall of Famer **Bobby Hull** was known for his blistering slap shot—but he also took a beating on the ice. Over his long career, Hull **lost 27 of his 30 teeth** due to high sticks, pucks to the face, and fights. When asked why he never wore a helmet or a visor, Hull simply shrugged and said, **"I need to see where I'm shooting."**

Mind-Blowing Hockey Fact #66

MIND-BLOWING HOCKEY FACT #66

THE PUCK THAT GOT STUCK IN A GOALIE'S PADS

An NHL puck **once disappeared inside a goalie's pads for nearly a minute!**

During a **2008 game**, Vancouver Canucks goalie **Roberto Luongo** made a routine save, but then something strange happened—the puck **vanished!** Players frantically searched the crease, the refs looked under Luongo, and even he had no idea where it was. After nearly a full minute of confusion, the puck was finally **found lodged inside his pads!**

Mind-Blowing Hockey Fact #67

MIND-BLOWING HOCKEY FACT #67

THE TIME A ZAMBONI DRIVER CRASHED INTO THE BOARDS

A Zamboni driver **once lost control and crashed straight into the boards!**

During a **2015 game**, fans at a minor league hockey game were left in shock when the **Zamboni driver accidentally hit the gas instead of the brakes.** The machine **slammed into the boards**, causing damage to the rink and **delaying the game for over 30 minutes.** Luckily, no one was hurt, but it remains one of the **wildest Zamboni mishaps in hockey history!**

Mind-Blowing Hockey Fact #68

MIND-BLOWING HOCKEY FACT #68

THE PLAYER WHO SCORED 10 POINTS IN ONE GAME

One NHL player **recorded an unbelievable 10 points in a single game!**

On **February 7, 1976, Darryl Sittler** of the Toronto Maple Leafs set an NHL record by scoring **six goals and adding four assists** for a total of **10 points in one game.** No player before or since has matched this jaw-dropping performance, making it one of the **most unbreakable records in hockey history.**

Mind-Blowing Hockey Fact #69

MIND-BLOWING HOCKEY FACT #69

THE COACH WHO BENCHED HIS ENTIRE TEAM

An NHL coach **once benched his entire team in the middle of a game!**

During a **1991 game**, legendary coach **Mike Keenan** of the Chicago Blackhawks was so furious with his team's poor effort that he **benched every single player on the roster.** He sent out only the fourth-line grinders and left his star players **sitting on the bench for nearly an entire period.** His bold move sent a clear message—and the Blackhawks responded by **winning the game!**

Mind-Blowing Hockey Fact #70

MIND-BLOWING HOCKEY FACT #70

THE FASTEST GOAL IN NHL HISTORY

An NHL player **once scored just two seconds into a game!**

On **December 19, 1984,** New York Islanders forward **Bryan Trottier** shocked everyone by scoring **just two seconds after the opening faceoff.** His lightning-fast goal remains the **fastest in NHL history**, proving that sometimes, all it takes is **one perfect shot to make history.**

Mind-Blowing Hockey Fact #71

MIND-BLOWING HOCKEY FACT #71

THE STANLEY CUP WAS DROP-KICKED OFF A BALCONY

An NHL player **once accidentally kicked the Stanley Cup off a balcony!**

After winning the **1991 Stanley Cup**, Pittsburgh Penguins forward **Mario Lemieux** hosted a celebration at his house. At some point during the party, a teammate jokingly tried to **drop-kick the Cup—but miscalculated and sent it flying off the balcony!** Luckily, the trophy survived the fall with only a few dents, proving that the **Stanley Cup is as tough as the players who win it!**

Mind-Blowing Hockey Fact #72

MIND-BLOWING HOCKEY FACT #72

THE LONGEST NHL SUSPENSION EVER

One NHL player **was suspended for a record-setting 41 games!**

In **2015**, **Raffi Torres** of the San Jose Sharks delivered a brutal hit to Anaheim Ducks forward **Jakob Silfverberg** during a preseason game. The NHL responded by **suspending Torres for 41 games**, the longest suspension for an on-ice incident in league history. The punishment sent a clear message about player safety, and Torres never played in the NHL again after serving his suspension.

Mind-Blowing Hockey Fact #73

MIND-BLOWING HOCKEY FACT #73

THE GOALIE WHO SCORED HIS OWN GOAL… IN OVERTIME

An NHL goalie **once lost a playoff game by accidentally scoring on himself in overtime!**

In **2013**, Phoenix Coyotes goalie **Mike Smith** had a nightmare moment when a harmless dump-in took a weird bounce off the boards. The puck hit the back of Smith's **legs**, trickled into the net, and **ended the game in overtime!** Since the last opposing player to touch the puck was awarded the goal, **Smith was officially credited with scoring against his own team!**

Mind-Blowing Hockey Fact #74

THE PLAYER WHO PLAYED WITHOUT A STICK

An NHL defenseman **once played an entire shift without a stick—and still made a save!**

During a **2008 game**, Detroit Red Wings defenseman **Niklas Kronwall** had his stick knocked out of his hands early in a shift. Instead of leaving the ice, he **kept playing without it**, using only his body to block shots and disrupt passes. At one point, he even **dove across the crease to stop a puck from going in**, making a save that would've made any goalie proud!

Mind-Blowing Hockey Fact #75

MIND-BLOWING HOCKEY FACT #75

THE REFEREE WHO FORGOT HIS WHISTLE

An NHL referee **once started a game without his whistle!**

During a **1996 game**, veteran referee **Kerry Fraser** skated onto the ice, dropped the puck for the opening faceoff—and then realized he **didn't have his whistle.** Play continued for several minutes as he **frantically searched his pockets**, before finally having to skate to the scorer's table to get a replacement. The moment left players and fans **laughing at the rare referee blunder.**

Mind-Blowing Hockey Fact #76

MIND-BLOWING HOCKEY FACT #76

THE PLAYER WHO PLAYED WITH A BROKEN SKATE

An NHL player **once finished a shift skating on one foot!**

During a **2014 game**, Boston Bruins forward **Brad Marchand** had his skate blade completely snap off after a collision. Instead of immediately leaving the ice, he **hopped around on one foot**, trying to stay in the play while waiting for a line change. The hilarious scene had fans and commentators **laughing as he struggled to keep his balance** before finally making it to the bench.

Mind-Blowing Hockey Fact #77

MIND-BLOWING HOCKEY FACT #77

THE PLAYER WHO FORGOT HIS JERSEY

An NHL player **once had to miss part of a game because he forgot his jersey!**

During a **2008 game**, Washington Capitals star **Alexander Ovechkin** was set to take the ice—until he realized **he had forgotten to bring his jersey to the bench.** The equipment staff scrambled to find it, but Ovechkin was forced to **sit out the start of the game** while they searched. When he finally got back on the ice, he made up for lost time by **scoring two goals!**

Mind-Blowing Hockey Fact #78

MIND-BLOWING HOCKEY FACT #78

THE GAME WITH NO STOPPAGES

An NHL period **once went 20 minutes without a single whistle!**

During a **2016 game** between the New York Rangers and Detroit Red Wings, the second period became one of the **smoothest in NHL history.** There were **no offside calls, no icings, no penalties, and no goals**—meaning the full 20-minute period was played without a single stoppage! Players later said it was one of the **fastest, most exhausting periods they had ever played.**

Mind-Blowing Hockey Fact #79

MIND-BLOWING HOCKEY FACT #79

THE PLAYER WHO SCORED 500 GOALS... WITHOUT A HAT TRICK

One NHL legend **scored over 500 career goals—but never had a hat trick!**

Hall of Famer **Gilbert Perreault** was one of the most consistent scorers in NHL history, netting **512 goals** in his career. But despite his offensive talent, he never once scored **three goals in a single game!** He holds the record for the **most career goals without ever recording a hat trick**, proving that **steady scoring can be just as legendary as explosive nights.**

Mind-Blowing Hockey Fact #80

MIND-BLOWING HOCKEY FACT #80

THE GOALIE WHO WORE THE WRONG JERSEY

An NHL goalie **once played an entire period wearing the wrong jersey!**

During a **2002 game**, New York Islanders backup goalie **Garth Snow** was forced into action when the starter got injured. In the rush to get on the ice, Snow **accidentally grabbed the wrong jersey**—one without his name or number! He played the entire period in the mystery jersey before the team **finally noticed and made him switch.**

Mind-Blowing Hockey Fact #81

MIND-BLOWING HOCKEY FACT #81

THE TIME THE PUCK GOT STUCK IN A GOALIE'S PANTS

An NHL game **once stopped because the puck vanished—inside a goalie's pants!**

During a **2017 game**, Toronto Maple Leafs goalie **Frederik Andersen** made a save, but the puck **completely disappeared.** Players searched the crease, referees looked around, and even Andersen was confused. After a long delay, the mystery was solved—the puck had somehow **slipped into his pants and was stuck in his pads the entire time!**

Mind-Blowing Hockey Fact #82

MIND-BLOWING HOCKEY FACT #82

THE TEAM THAT WON A GAME WITHOUT TAKING A SHOT

An NHL team **once won a game in overtime without recording a single shot!**

During a **2014 game,** the Arizona Coyotes and Buffalo Sabres were tied heading into overtime. Just seconds into the extra frame, a Sabres defenseman **accidentally knocked the puck into his own net** while attempting a pass. Since the Coyotes never actually shot the puck, they **won the game without officially registering a shot in overtime!**

Mind-Blowing Hockey Fact #83

MIND-BLOWING HOCKEY FACT #83

THE GAME WITH THREE GOALIE ASSISTS

An NHL goalie **once recorded three assists in a single game!**

On **March 22, 1984**, Edmonton Oilers goalie **Grant Fuhr** made history by registering **three assists** in a game against the Minnesota North Stars. While goalies rarely pick up points, Fuhr was known for his ability to **play the puck and start breakouts**. His three-assist night remains a record for **the most assists by a goalie in a single game**.

Mind-Blowing Hockey Fact #84

MIND-BLOWING HOCKEY FACT #84

THE PLAYER WHO PLAYED FOR TWO TEAMS IN ONE PLAYOFF

One NHL player **played for two different teams in the same playoffs!**

In **1980**, forward **Ken Linseman** started the postseason with the **Philadelphia Flyers**, but after an early-round exit, he was **sent to the AHL on a minor-league assignment.** However, because of a unique rule at the time, he was then **called up by the Edmonton Oilers**, who were still in the playoffs! Linseman remains one of the **only players to ever compete for two different teams in a single postseason.**

Mind-Blowing Hockey Fact #85

MIND-BLOWING HOCKEY FACT #85

THE FASTEST FOUR GOALS IN NHL HISTORY

An NHL team **once scored four goals in just 49 seconds!**

On **March 19, 1944**, the **Montreal Canadiens** set an unbreakable record by scoring **four goals in just 49 seconds** against the New York Rangers. The explosion of offense happened so fast that even the arena announcer **couldn't keep up with calling the goals!** To this day, no team has been able to match this **lightning-fast scoring streak.**

Mind-Blowing Hockey Fact #86

MIND-BLOWING HOCKEY FACT #86

THE PLAYER WHO PLAYED WITH A BROKEN JAW

An NHL player **once finished a game with a broken jaw—then played the next game too!**

During the **1964 Stanley Cup Final**, Toronto Maple Leafs forward **Bobby Baun** took a slap shot to the face, breaking his jaw. Instead of leaving the game, he **had it frozen with painkillers and returned to the ice.** Not only did he finish the game, but he played again **two nights later**, helping the Leafs win the Cup. His toughness remains one of the most legendary moments in NHL history!

Mind-Blowing Hockey Fact #87

MIND-BLOWING HOCKEY FACT #87

THE TIME AN NHL GAME WAS DELAYED BY A BAT

An NHL game **was once stopped because of a live bat flying around the rink!**

During a **1975 playoff game** between the Buffalo Sabres and the Philadelphia Flyers, a bat began **swooping over the ice**, distracting players and fans. After multiple failed attempts to shoo it away, Sabres forward **Jim Lorentz** took matters into his own hands—literally—by **swatting the bat out of midair with his stick!** The bizarre moment remains one of the strangest delays in NHL history.

Mind-Blowing Hockey Fact #88

MIND-BLOWING HOCKEY FACT #88

THE TEAM THAT SCORED ON THEIR OWN EMPTY NET

An NHL team **once pulled their goalie—and accidentally scored on themselves!**

During a **2013 game**, the **Buffalo Sabres** were on a delayed penalty call, meaning the play would stop once the other team touched the puck. To gain an extra attacker, the Sabres **pulled their goalie**—but then a misplayed pass went all the way down the ice and into their own empty net! Since no opposing player touched the puck, **the goal was credited to the last Sabres player who had possession!**

Mind-Blowing Hockey Fact #89

THE PLAYER WHO TOOK A PENALTY WHILE ON THE BENCH

An NHL player **once got a penalty—while sitting on the bench!**

During a **1991 game**, the Detroit Red Wings' **Bob Probert** was chirping at the referees from the bench when he took things too far. The official **turned around and gave him a two-minute penalty**, forcing Detroit to play shorthanded. Getting a penalty without even being on the ice remains one of the rarest infractions in NHL history!

Mind-Blowing Hockey Fact #90

MIND-BLOWING HOCKEY FACT #90

THE TIME A GOALIE PLAYED WITHOUT A MASK

An NHL goalie **once played in the modern era without a mask—by accident!**

During a **1973 game**, Philadelphia Flyers goalie **Doug Favell** was warming up when his mask **accidentally broke just before puck drop.** With no backup available, he had **no choice but to start the game maskless!** He played the first period without protection before finally getting a replacement. It was one of the last times a goalie ever faced NHL shots without a mask!

＃ Mind-Blowing Hockey Fact #91

MIND-BLOWING HOCKEY FACT #91

THE PLAYER WHO SCORED WHILE SITTING DOWN

An NHL player **once scored a goal while sitting on the ice!**

During a **2006 game**, Pittsburgh Penguins forward **Evgeni Malkin** was knocked down while driving to the net. Instead of giving up on the play, he **swung his stick while sitting on the ice and somehow fired the puck into the goal!** The incredible effort left fans and commentators in awe, proving that **Malkin could score from anywhere.**

Mind-Blowing Hockey Fact #92

MIND-BLOWING HOCKEY FACT #92

THE GAME THAT ENDED IN FOG

An NHL playoff game **was once stopped because of thick fog covering the ice!**

During **Game 3 of the 1975 Stanley Cup Final**, the Buffalo Sabres and Philadelphia Flyers faced an unexpected challenge—**fog so dense that players could barely see the puck!** With no way to clear the rink, officials had to pause the game **multiple times** to let the fog settle. The bizarre conditions didn't stop Buffalo from winning, but the game became known as "The Fog Game"—one of the strangest in NHL history.

Mind-Blowing Hockey Fact #93

MIND-BLOWING HOCKEY FACT #93

THE GOALIE WHO PLAYED WITHOUT A STICK

An NHL goalie **once finished a game without his stick!**

During a **2008 game**, New Jersey Devils goalie **Martin Brodeur** lost his stick after a collision near the net. With no time to retrieve it, he **played the final two minutes using only his pads and blocker to make saves.** Despite the disadvantage, he still managed to **shut down the opposing team and secure the win!**

Mind-Blowing Hockey Fact #94

MIND-BLOWING HOCKEY FACT #94

THE PLAYER WHO SCORED ON HIS OWN PENALTY SHOT

An NHL player **once missed a penalty shot—but still scored anyway!**

During a **2011 game**, Anaheim Ducks forward **Bobby Ryan** took a penalty shot but lost control of the puck before getting a shot off. Frustrated, he circled back, stole the puck from the defending player, and **scored seconds later in the regular play!** While the penalty shot itself didn't count, Ryan still got the last laugh by putting the puck in the net right after.

Mind-Blowing Hockey Fact #95

MIND-BLOWING HOCKEY FACT #95

THE TIME A PLAYER SCORED A GOAL WITH HIS HEAD

An NHL player **once scored a goal by accidentally using his head!**

During a **2010 game**, Phoenix Coyotes forward **Shane Doan** was battling in front of the net when a teammate's shot **deflected off his helmet and into the goal.** The puck never touched his stick, but since it wasn't a deliberate head-butt, the goal **counted!** It remains one of the most bizarre ways a player has ever put the puck in the net.

Mind-Blowing Hockey Fact #96

MIND-BLOWING HOCKEY FACT #96

THE TIME A PLAYER SCORED WITH A BROKEN STICK

An NHL player **once scored a goal even though his stick was broken!**

During a **2007 game**, Pittsburgh Penguins star **Sidney Crosby** took a slap shot just as his stick **snapped in half.** The puck still had enough momentum to **fly past the goalie and into the net!** Since the shot was taken **before** the stick fully broke, the goal was legal, making it one of the most unique goals in NHL history.

Mind-Blowing Hockey Fact #97

MIND-BLOWING HOCKEY FACT #97

THE PLAYER WHO SCORED FIVE GOALS FIVE DIFFERENT WAYS

An NHL player **once scored five goals in a single game—each in a completely different way!**

On **December 31, 1988, Mario Lemieux** of the Pittsburgh Penguins pulled off one of the most incredible feats in hockey history. He found the back of the net at **even strength, on the power play, shorthanded, on a penalty shot, and into an empty net.** No other player has ever matched this **one-of-a-kind scoring achievement!**

Mind-Blowing Hockey Fact #98

MIND-BLOWING HOCKEY FACT #98

THE GAME THAT LASTED THREE DAYS

One NHL playoff game **took so long to finish that it stretched over three calendar days!**

During the **1936 Stanley Cup Playoffs**, the Detroit Red Wings and Montreal Maroons battled through an exhausting **six overtime periods**, making it the longest game in NHL history. The marathon matchup lasted **176 minutes and 30 seconds** before Mud Bruneteau finally scored the game-winning goal. By the time it ended, players were completely drained, and the game had officially crossed into its **third day!**

Mind-Blowing Hockey Fact #99

MIND-BLOWING HOCKEY FACT #99

THE PLAYER WHO SCORED HIS FIRST GOAL INTO HIS OWN NET

An NHL rookie **scored his first-ever NHL goal—against his own team!**

During a **2013 game**, Calgary Flames defenseman **Dennis Wideman** was trying to clear the puck from his own zone when he accidentally **fired it straight into his own net.** Since no opposing player had touched the puck, the goal was officially credited to the last player on the other team who had possession. Wideman eventually scored plenty of goals the right way, but his **first NHL "goal" was one he'd rather forget!**

Mind-Blowing Hockey Fact #100

MIND-BLOWING HOCKEY FACT #100

THE STANLEY CUP THAT GOT LEFT AT THE AIRPORT

The Stanley Cup **was once forgotten at an airport baggage claim!**

After winning the Cup in **1924**, the Montreal Canadiens were on their way to a victory celebration when they **stopped to change a flat tire.** The players took the Cup out of the car to make room, but when they drove off, they **accidentally left it on the side of the road!** Hours later, they rushed back and found it **still sitting there—completely untouched!**

CONCLUSION

Congratulations! You've just powered through **100 Mind-Blowing Hockey Facts**, uncovering the wild, unpredictable, and downright unbelievable moments that make this sport so legendary. From **bizarre bloopers** to **record-breaking feats**, these stories prove that hockey is much more than just a game—it's a world of **chaos, skill, and surprises** waiting to unfold.

But here's the thing about hockey—it never stops evolving. For every fact you've read, there are countless more waiting to happen, each adding to the sport's **rich and unpredictable history.** Maybe this book has deepened your love for hockey, given you a new appreciation for its **crazy moments**, or simply reminded you why it's one of the most **exciting sports on the planet.**

The truth is, **hockey's greatest stories** aren't just in the past—they're happening every night on the ice. Whether you're watching from the stands, following from home, or lacing up your own skates, the next **mind-blowing moment** could be just one shift away.

So as you close this book, don't think of it as the final buzzer—think of it as the start of **overtime,** where the best moments are still waiting to be written.

Until next time, **stay curious, stay passionate, and remember—hockey will always find new ways to blow your mind.**

ACKNOWLEDGEMENTS

Creating **100 Mind-Blowing Hockey Facts** has been a journey filled with passion, dedication, and a whole lot of appreciation for the **wildest sport on ice.** While my name may be on the cover, this book wouldn't have come to life without the support, inspiration, and enthusiasm of so many incredible people.

First, a huge thank you to the **hockey fans, historians, and trivia lovers** who have shared legendary stories from the game's rich history. Your passion for the sport and its **crazy, unpredictable moments** has been a constant source of inspiration, and this book is a celebration of those unbelievable tales.

To my **family and friends,** who have patiently listened to my endless chatter about **miracle goals, record-breaking moments, and Zamboni mishaps**—you are the real MVPs. Your encouragement and enthusiasm helped fuel this project every step of the way.

A special shoutout to my **readers**—you are the reason this book exists! Whether you're here for the **laughs, the jaw-dropping moments, or the ultimate hockey trivia**, this book is for you. Your curiosity and love for the game keep these incredible hockey stories alive.

And finally, to the game of **hockey itself**—thank you for being so **fast, unpredictable, and full of surprises.** You've gifted us with moments that will **never be forgotten,** and I'm beyond grateful for the opportunity to share just a few of them.

Here's to **hockey, to the legends of the past, and to the unbelievable stories still waiting to be written.**

ABOUT THE AUTHOR

Felix Grayson is a storyteller at heart, driven by an **insatiable curiosity for the strange, surprising, and downright unpredictable moments in sports.** With a passion for uncovering the wildest and most unbelievable tales from the world of **hockey**, Felix has crafted **100 Mind-Blowing Hockey Facts** to entertain, amaze, and spark wonder in fans of all ages.

When he's not **digging through archives** or chasing down the next **quirky hockey moment,** Felix enjoys watching games from **rink-side seats, revisiting legendary hockey documentaries, and debating the greatest goals, fights, and comebacks** over a hot drink at the arena. A firm believer in the magic of the sport and the power of a good story, Felix invites you to take this journey through **hockey's most unbelievable moments, proving that the game is just as full of surprises off the ice as it is on.**

www.ingramcontent.com/pod-product-compliance
Lightning Source LLC
Chambersburg PA
CBHW030318080526
44584CB00012B/616